REAL WORLD ECONOMICS™

Understanding
Economic
Indicators
Predicting Future Trends in the Economy

KATHY FURGANG

ROSEN
PUBLISHING®

New York

Published in 2012 by The Rosen Publishing Group, Inc.
29 East 21st Street, New York, NY 10010

Library of Congress Cataloging-in-Publication Data

Furgang, Kathy.
Understanding economic indicators: predicting future trends in the
economy/Kathy Furgang.—1st ed.
     p. cm.—(Real world economics)
Includes bibliographical references and index.
ISBN 978-1-4488-5571-1 (library binding)
1. Economic indicators—Juvenile literature. 2. Gross domestic product—
Juvenile literature. I. Title.
HC59.3.F87 2012

330.01'5195—dc23

330.01

FUR

2011017461

Manufactured in China

CPSIA Compliance Information: Batch #W12YA: For further information, contact Rosen Publishing, New York, New York, at
1-800-237-9932.

On the cover: Housing starts—the construction of new houses and
apartment buildings—are considered a leading indicator of economic
health and vitality.

Contents

INTRODUCTION

They say "Money makes the world go round." In some ways, it certainly does. If you are sharp-eyed enough to notice, there are signs everywhere that tell you how well or poorly the world of money is going around. Sometimes these signs are quite literal. Signs like "For Sale—Price Reduced," "Going Out of Business," or "Store Closed" generally point to an economy that is in poor health. Conversely, signs that declare "Now Hiring," "Grand Opening," and "Sold" indicate that the economy is growing.

Other signs of economic health are not so obvious. They include the length of time it takes for a house to sell, how long a new store stays open, or how long it takes to rent a vacant space where an old business used to be. You may see construction projects that get halted for months. You may see long lines at an unemployment office. You may see no one taking advantage of huge sales at the mall. Even at home there are

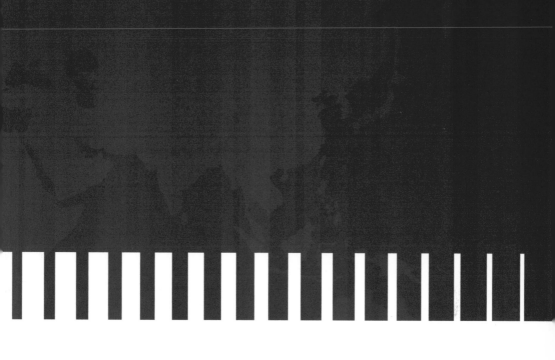

Many closed storefronts in a neighborhood may be a sign that the economy is struggling.

signs of the state of the economy's health. Some families cannot afford to go on vacation like they normally do.

These are all signs that the economy, or the wealth of a country or region, is growing (doing well) or contracting (not doing well). All of these signs of economic activity or non-activity are part of a large group of statistics and data known as economic indicators. People who study the economy know that these signs cannot only be detected, but they can also be measured and analyzed. Definitive and insightful statements regarding the present state of the economy can be made based on analysis of economic indicators. So, too, can predictions about the future performance of the economy. Economists use these economic indicators to confirm the present state of the economy—whether it is growing or shrinking—and anticipate whether the economy will continue to grow or shrink in the near future.

There are natural and cyclical trends in the economy, which tends to alternate between periods of growth and recession. With the help of economic data and the analysis of economic indicators, economists can locate the economy's present position within the cycle and anticipate its next movements. They can let the government and ordinary citizens know when the nation may be entering an economic downturn and when improvement and renewed growth can be expected. Let's find out how economists "read the signs" and come up with solid data that provides reliable and accurate information about the upward or downward direction in which the economy is headed.

CHAPTER ONE
THE THREE TYPES OF ECONOMIC INDICATORS

The Great Recession of 2007–2009 hit Americans very hard. But it didn't start out as the "Great Recession." In fact, it took years to get to that point. The recession began in 2007, but it came as no surprise to economists. There were signs for years that the economy would be headed for a decline. But how could economists know that things were starting to go badly? And how did some of these economists anticipate just how dire things would get before the economy began a very gradual and halting recovery? What kind of economic indicators did they study, and how did they interpret this information?

The economists collected data associated with the three types of economic indicators: leading (preceding movements of the economic cycle), lagging (manifesting themselves after the major movements of the economic cycle), and coincident (reflecting the present state of the economic cycle). They then analyzed this data and came to solid and accurate conclusions about what condition the economy was in at present, the degree to which it would worsen, the likely duration of the recession, and the probable timing and pace of the recovery.

Leading Economic Indicators

The first of the three economic indicators are leading economic indicators. These are economic conditions or activities that change before the economy changes. Even when the economy may seem perfectly sound to most people, conditions may be changing in certain sectors of the economy. This provides an early signal of a looming slowdown.

One way the economy can change is if production in one specific sector may develop. For example, before the Great Recession, there was a huge boom in the real estate industry. New homes were being built in many places around the country. At first, demand was outstripping the ever-increasing supply of homes. People were buying the newly constructed houses, and developers and realtors were making money building and selling the homes. Eventually, however, there were more houses on the market than there were interested buyers. The result was a housing glut.

A big boom in one industry or another—sometimes referred to as a bubble—is a leading economic indicator. Booms occur before the economy actually changes. The very existence of the boom is a sign that it will one day end, or the bubble will burst,

New construction often indicates that an economy is booming.

perhaps sooner rather than later. In the context of the housing boom, this meant that construction eventually slowed and then virtually halted. This led to unemployment in the construction and building materials sector of the economy. With a large supply of houses and little demand, housing prices sagged nationwide. This negatively affected even those homeowners who had not taken part in the frenzied buying and selling of recent years. Some home values dropped so much that people owed more on their housing loans than the homes were actually worth. All of these downward trends drained cash from the economy and made individuals and businesses very cautious about spending, thereby further draining the economy of money. The recession was on.

At the time a bubble is occurring, most people are not thinking about future consequences. They are just content to benefit from the boom and are not inclined to analyze the situation more closely or look forward to the inevitable bust. Economists, however, are trained to peer into the economic future and identify emerging trends. They gather statistics about the number of houses being built and the raw materials needed to build those houses. They even keep track of the exact areas where new construction is occurring. They then get information on the percentage of increase in new housing construction in any given area. They know that a boom is not a random event or one that only has relevance in the present. It will have consequences for the future as well, and those future ripple effects can lead the economy into a recession.

For example, when housing supply exceeds demand, sales slow down. That means that real estate agencies may lay off employees because fewer agents are needed to sell homes. Construction companies may also lay off workers because new home construction has slowed. There may be a lot of home building materials, such as wood, plastic, or metals that are not selling, so supply stores may begin to suffer. In this way, some industries feel the pinch of the bubble bursting before others do. It may take years before the ripple effects of a housing slowdown reach the rest of the economy.

Even though average citizens do not often pay attention to them, small signs of change in the economy, such as an uptick in initial unemployment claims, can indicate to economists that big changes are not too far behind.

COINCIDENT ECONOMIC INDICATORS

Another kind of economic indicator is a coincident economic indicator. This refers to the economic conditions or activities that reflect the present state of the economy (rather than its past or likely future states). Over time, leading economic indicators—those that alert economists to future economic trends—have a ripple effect throughout the rest of the economy. The initially limited impact of layoffs in the areas of real estate and construction, for example, begin to affect other segments of the economy—and more and more people—months later.

When people are out of work, they cannot afford to buy new clothes or items for their homes. They can't afford to go on vacation. They can't afford to make improvements to their homes or go out to eat. This affects all of the other industries, such as retail stores, plumbing and remodeling companies, travel destinations, restaurants, and other places where people spend their income. As a result, layoffs are eventually needed in these industries, too, and the unemployment rate begins to rise more quickly and noticeably.

After an economy has slowed, there are lasting effects on a community. Many people do not have extra money for luxuries like dining out.

The unemployment rate is one of the most important and telling coincident economic indicators. When the economy is strong, the unemployment rate is low. When the economy is weak or weakening, the unemployment rate begins to climb. The unemployment rate helps signal where the economy is within the business cycle—peak, recession, trough (when the economy hits bottom), or recovery.

Lagging Economic Indicators

It takes a while for a decline in the economy to take effect—and even longer for the decline to be clearly manifested throughout the economy. A recovery may also be slow to occur, expand throughout most sectors of the economy, and become apparent to the general public. A lagging economic indicator is one that becomes apparent only after the economy has emerged into a new phase of the business cycle. It reflects the economy's previous position in that cycle.

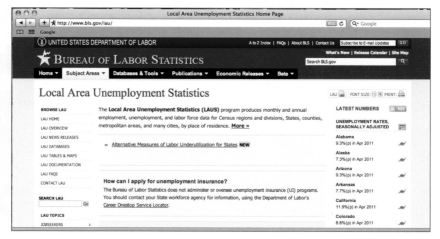

Unemployment data is updated each month by the Bureau of Labor Statistics (http://www.bls.gov). These figures indicate how many people are out of work nationwide and within specific regions and localities.

An example of a lagging economic indicator is the length of time that the unemployment rate stays at a certain level. During the Great Recession, the unemployment rate surpassed 10 percent. This means that one in ten working Americans was out of work. But a more telling indicator of the economy was how long it took for that rate to decline again. Even when the economy is improving and businesses are beginning to produce and sell more goods and services again, that does not necessarily mean that they can afford to hire back the same number of people they had before the recession. After a recession, companies spend their money cautiously. They are fearful that the economy will slip back into the doldrums without a recovery taking firm hold. They may hire temporary or part-time workers first. Or they may attempt to increase production without any new hiring, whether temporary or permanent, part-time or full-time.

So even when the economy is slowly improving, the unemployment rate remains high for a period, until business owners feel more confident in the recovery and optimistic about future prospects. Economists keep track of how long the unemployment rate stays high. The amount of time it takes an economy to recover is a lagging economic indicator. The statistic that measures this is the number of people who have been unemployed for six months or more, or over a year, or even over two or more years.

Economists are always looking at reports that show measures of the economy, such as the unemployment rate, the hiring rate, the rate of increase in pay, and the amount of goods being produced in different industries. Together, these statistics give a clearer picture of the economy—where it was six months ago, where it is now, and where it might be headed in the near future.

CHAPTER TWO

LEADING ECONOMIC INDICATORS

In order to get a snapshot of the relative health of the economy, the most important economic indicator to consider is the gross domestic product, or GDP. The GDP is the total value of goods and services produced within a country during a given period of time (usually a year). The GDP of the United States is measured both quarterly (four times a year) and annually (at year's end).

The GDP

The GDP is the most important indicator of how fast or slow an economy is growing. It is the percentage change in the GDP that makes economists understand how the economy is changing. The reason that the GDP is so important is that it accounts for all the goods manufactured and services performed during a specific time period. This detailed accounting provides a sharp and accurate portrait of current economic activity.

Service industries such as restaurants are included when the gross domestic product is calculated.

Services include people working in the tourist and travel industries, the entertainment and food industries, and the building and construction industries. The goods produced are the things that people make. This includes everything from paper and books to steel and buildings. If the GDP starts to decrease, this means that the value of a nation's goods and services has dropped, as has its productivity. This loss of value is a leading economic indicator for the downward movement of the entire economy.

New Orders for Durable Goods, Shipments, and Inventories

A durable good is an item that does not wear out quickly and thus does not need to be replaced very often. Items such as cars,

17

refrigerators and other home appliances, electronics, sports equipment, furniture, toys, computers, cell phones, and jewelry are all durable goods. When people buy these goods, they do not expect to have to replace them for several years. Keeping track of how many people are buying these items gives a good indication about the health of the economy. For example, if the economy is doing well (or consumers think it will continue to do well), people often have the income and confidence to buy a new car or a new sofa. But when the economy is not doing well (or consumers fear it will not be doing well in the near future), people tend to make do with what they have until another time when they may have more money.

One way economists determine how the sales of durable goods change is by looking at the numbers related to shipments of these goods. They also look at the inventory of goods in warehouses. An inventory is the exact number of particular items in a store or warehouse. A full warehouse with low rates of shipping indicates that the goods are not selling quickly. However, when a company can't keep store shelves stocked, its warehouses are empty, and it awaits delivery of more high-demand goods from the manufacturer or supplier, that's a good indication of a healthy economy.

Electronics are considered durable goods because they last more than a few years. An increase in sales of durable goods is an indicator of a healthy or growing economy.

When the sale of durable goods slows down, the manufacture of these goods also slows down. The oversupply of goods is brought in line with the lower demand. When an economy begins to slow down, sales of the most expensive manufactured items—cars, boats, designer clothes, and luxury goods—decrease. Conversely, an increase in new orders and shipments of durable goods are an indication that an economy is improving and growing. After years of putting off the purchase of that new car, a family may begin to feel confident enough in their finances and in the future prospects of the economy to devote money to such a big-ticket item. In this way, an increase in sales of durable goods is a leading indicator of an economy's return to health and a period of growth.

Average Manufacturer's Workweek

The average hours that manufacturers keep their factories in operation during a week can also indicate changes in an economy and its relative state of health. If a slowdown in durable goods orders occurs, the factory would be wise to slow down production of the goods in order to avoid oversupply during a period of low demand. That means possible layoffs or a reduction in employees' work hours. Conversely, an increase in the average weekly hours that a factory is open and operating provides an important indication of economic improvement and growth.

But the increase in workweek hours of one manufacturer would not be enough to make economists conclude that a positive change is coming to the economy. An overall increase among many different types of manufacturers would be required for economists to feel confident that the economy

When not enough goods are sold and manufactured, some factories cannot stay open, and jobs are lost.

was recovering and growing. If retailers are suddenly placing more orders for cars, washing machines, computers, and furniture from manufacturers, this broad-based surge in demand and production could reliably indicate a positive trend in the overall economy.

CONSTRUCTION AND HOUSING

Construction and housing have always been important indicators of the economy's health. That's because housing is probably the most expensive purchase most people will make in their lives. If houses sell at a brisk pace, it means a large number of people feel they have enough money—and are likely to continue making enough money in the future—to make such a large and expensive purchase and long-term financial commitment.

Similarly, if homes and buildings are being constructed in large numbers, it indicates that developers and investors have enough money to sink into building projects. It also means that there is a perceived demand for the new supply of housing and office and retail space. The ups and downs of the housing market and the construction of new buildings are what economists always keep a sharp eye on when determining the direction the economy is heading.

CONSTRUCTION SPENDING

When the amount of money spent on construction increases, it usually means that investors think they can make a profit from the building projects in which they invest. An investor is someone

Government Bailouts

Just like an ordinary individual, when a large corporation experiences tough economic times, it may need some government help to get by. Governments all around the world have given help, or bailouts, to companies in danger of failing and going bankrupt. The government typically offers this help when it feels that the company's failure would have such a profound impact on the economy that it would create or worsen a recession or even lead to a collapse of the financial system itself.

In the case of the United States, a government bailout was given to automobile companies that had approached the brink of bankruptcy due to extremely low sales, plunging revenue, escalating costs, and massive layoffs. General Motors (GM) was one of the companies that received a government bailout in 2008. By 2010, the company was again operating at a profit and was able to pay back some of the money it had been given by the government.

While government bailouts are a major indicator of economic trouble, it is what happens after the bailout that could be a true indicator of an economy's strength. If the money spent on the struggling businesses prevents failure and promotes a return to profitability and renewed hiring, the money can be said to have been well spent. The government has invested in the nation's future, and everyone reaps the dividends.

who spends money in hopes of getting a profit in return. If an investor spends money on constructing houses, for example, the investor thinks that he or she will be able to sell the houses for a profit once they are built. An increase in construction spending usually indicates a strong or strengthening economy.

A decrease in construction spending means that investors do not feel that they could make money on the investment. They either don't think new buildings will sell because of a poor economy, or they feel that an area already has enough buildings. As a result, they withhold their money from building projects, and construction is either halted or never begins in the first place.

Housing Starts and Building Permits

Before a house, housing development, apartment or office building, or retail space is built, a public record is made of the project. The number of building permits issued by a town or city is something measurable. Economists can use these public records to find out which areas of the nation are experiencing an increase in new construction. They can also use building permit information to identify any unusually long gaps in construction time between a project's groundbreaking and its completion. An unusually long time between the beginning and end of a project might indicate that at some point the builders ran out of money. They had to halt construction until new investors were lined up or new funds were otherwise raised.

Analyzing the time that elapses between building starts and completions can offer unique insights into the relative health of the development company in charge of the project, the local economy, and perhaps, the larger national economy. If there seems to be a national trend of quick building completions or slow and protracted building completions, conclusions can be made about the health of the national economy. Building projects that are finished quickly show that there is a great demand for the homes, offices, or retail spaces being constructed and plenty of investor cash funding the effort. Conversely, building projects that are put on hold indicate that there is a low demand for the homes, offices, or retail spaces. As a result, investors have pulled out, or the money for the project has run out for some reason that most likely reflects a slowing and shrinking economy.

NEW HOME SALES

After tracking home starts—the beginning of construction on new homes and housing developments—the next statistic economists turn to is new house sales. The homes have been built, but are they selling? It would be wonderful if every home that is built has an owner ready and waiting for it. However, this is not always the case. In fact, even economists admit that it is difficult to determine when a housing market has reached a bubble—when the supply begins to outpace the demand. In other words, it is hard to tell when more homes have been made than are really needed or desired.

In the years before the Great Recession, it became increasingly clear that the building boom had outstripped the actual demand for housing. Before funding any more development projects, banks wanted to make sure that home sales were keeping pace with new home construction. In order to boost lagging demand for a growing housing supply, the banks began to offer mortgages to people who would ordinarily not have qualified for a home loan. They would not have qualified because they had a poor credit rating and a low income. Ordinarily, they would have been considered a bad loan risk. During the housing bubble, however, some borrowers were allowed to buy homes that were well out of their price range.

While this was a short-term fix to the housing oversupply problem and helped boost home sales, it inadvertently caused a chain reaction of negative developments that plunged the nation—and the world—into an extremely severe and long-lasting recession.

Housing Vacancies and Home Ownerships

By making loans easily available, even to those who were poor risks and first-time homeowners, the banks had successfully boosted demand in a housing market that had threatened to be glutted by unsold homes. Yet many of these new homeowners and subprime borrowers were having trouble making their monthly mortgage payments. Many people could no longer afford to keep the homes they had purchased, either because the monthly payments were too high or because they had been laid off—or both.

BANK

(6) 3 BEDR

- ELEGANT & SPACIO
- CLOSED CIRCUIT C
- QUALITY LAMINATE
- KITCHENS W/CUSTO
- STAINLESS STEEL AP

More and more people had to foreclose on their homes. That meant that the bank had to take possession of the houses that people could not afford to pay for anymore. The number of foreclosures in 2007 sharply increased by 75 percent.

Problems in the housing market—including slow sales, mortgage defaults, and foreclosures—were a leading economic indicator of the Great Recession of 2007–09.

The next year it spiked another 112 percent from the year before. By 2009, the foreclosures in the United States had reached an all-time high, jumping another 23 percent over 2008 levels.

Hundreds of thousands of families were forced to leave their homes in the wake of the burst housing bubble. The number of home vacancies and bank foreclosures on homes is one of the most revealing—and chilling—leading economic indicators of a recession or of an even more severe economic depression.

STOCK MARKET RETURNS

"Stock market return" is a term that refers to the profitability of stocks and the amount of money an investor earns on each share that he or she purchases. The more a share is worth, the more profit the stockholder will receive when he or she sells the stock. During times of economic growth, stock prices are generally high. However, gloomy economic reports, disappointing corporate profits, political uncertainty, global instability,

natural disasters or emergencies, and plain old investor panic can cause stock prices to fall.

Economists chart the rise and fall of the stock market by examining various stock indexes—collections of certain stocks

The performance of the stock market is an important leading economic indicator. The stock market crash of 2008 was the worst since the Great Depression.

that represent the leading companies in their fields. One such index is the S&P 500. This index was introduced in the 1920s by a financial company called Standard & Poors. It keeps track of five hundred major companies and the performance of their stocks. For instance, the stock market crash of 2008 caused the S&P 500 to fall 38.6 percent that year. That was the index's worst performance since the Great Depression. The next year, things were already looking brighter on Wall Street with a 23.5 percent gain for the S&P 500 in 2009. Even so, the S&P 500 was down 15 percent from its 2007 high. The index continued to rise in 2010, with a 13 percent gain.

Other leading stock market indices include the Dow Jones Industrial Average, the NASDAQ Composite, and the Nikkei 225. Some stock market indices are devoted to companies that specialize in energy, electronics, the environment and clean energy, water, finance, raw materials, metals, technology, real estate, and even space technology.

Money Supply

The money supply is the total amount of money available in an economy at any given time. When the money supply is high, prices may rise as well. This is because so much cash is circulating throughout the economy that companies and stores feel comfortable raising their prices. They assume that people have enough money on hand to pay extra. When price inflation occurs, banks try to "cool" the economy by draining it of

As chairman of the Federal Reserve during the Great Recession, Ben Bernanke crafted monetary policies designed to increase the flow of money through the cash-starved economy.

some cash. This is known as reducing the money supply. It is achieved by raising interest rates, making it more expensive for businesses and individuals to borrow money.

The Federal Reserve is the central bank of the United States, and it dictates the monetary policies for the country and the size of its money supply. The decisions made by the Federal Reserve affect the interest rates people are charged for loans. They also affect the interest rates that govern people's savings accounts, determining how much their savings grow over time after being deposited in the bank. In addition, the decisions of the Federal Reserve affect the value of the dollar around the world. When the money supply is high, the value of the dollar—how much it can buy—tends to drop. The dollar's value increases when the supply is lower.

The Federal Reserve works to keep the economy as stable as possible. Economic indicators that seem to signal a quickly growing economy or a shrinking economy help the Fed decide if any changes to the money supply need to be made to avoid either recession or inflation and to sustain steady growth.

INTERNATIONAL TRADE AND TRANSACTIONS

The United States is not alone in the world, nor does it possess a self-sufficient economy. In order to obtain everything it needs for its citizens, businesses, and industries, it must trade with other countries. It also must engage in trade in order to sell overseas what it produces. International trade boosts revenue and generates wealth throughout society.

Statistics associated with international trade provide economists with insights about not only the health of the American economy, but the global economy as well. As the Great Recession vividly illustrated, all the worlds' economies are linked by globalization, and trouble in one spells trouble for all.

Suppose American sales of durable goods such as cars start to slow—a leading indicator of a shrinking economy. This means that orders for cars made at overseas factories will also slow down. This, in turn, negatively affects international trade. If the nations that make the cars Americans are no longer demanding receive less revenue through trade, their economies suffer. Foreign car manufacturers may lay off workers. Foreign consumers will begin spending less as their economies slow, which means that the purchase of American goods by foreign nations will drop. This leads to American layoffs and further reductions in spending and consumer activity. Lower consumer spending results in even more layoffs, and a vicious global cycle is underway.

Consumer Confidence Index

The Consumer Confidence Index is a measure of how people feel about the direction in which the economy is headed, based upon their saving and spending attitudes and patterns. If people have been laid off from their jobs or if they notice that many people around them have been laid off, their confidence in the economy drops, as does their spending. Typically, their level of saving increases during these periods of low consumer confidence.

When an increasing number of people choose to put their money in the bank, it often means that the economy is not making them feel confident about the future. They are afraid to spend money in case they lose their job, so they save it instead in an effort to build up reserves in case of a financial emergency.

To create the index, the Conference Board, an independent economic research group, sends out surveys every month to five thousand American households. The survey consists of only five questions regarding respondents' opinions on current business conditions, business conditions for the next six months, current employment conditions, employment conditions for the next six months, and total family income for the next six months. It can be taken each month to chart the changes in people's attitudes about the economy.

During 2008, the Consumer Confidence Index dropped and continued to slip throughout the year. In May of 2008, it hit a sixteen-year low. In just that one month, it had fallen to 57.2 from 62.8. And things were about to get even worse. By February of 2009, the Consumer Confidence Index dropped to 25 from the 37.4 the month before.

When consumer confidence is low, that indicates to economists that consumers do not have—or don't feel that they have—any money to put into the economy. Instead, any available cash goes into savings as a hedge against economic and job insecurity. That means that people won't be buying durable goods, eating out, taking vacations, or spending money on anything else they'd ordinarily spend it on in a healthy economy.

By 2010 and early 2011, the Consumer Confidence Index was again increasing. However, it only returned to 2008 levels, when consumer confidence had already been battered by the recession. This shows that even if economists tell the public that a recovery is underway, consumers don't necessarily feel confident enough to put their money back into the economy by buying goods and services.

The Consumer Sentiment Index is another monthly index that measures people's attitudes about the economy and their own personal finances through a fifty-question survey. It has been published monthly by the University of Michigan since 1964. Following a pattern similar to the Consumer Confidence

Index, the Consumer Sentiment Index dipped during 2008 and then sank to historic lows in 2009.

Consumer confidence can often lag behind actual economic improvement. Generally, business and industry feel the effects of a growing economy and regain their confidence before the average person enjoys greater wealth, job security, and growing confidence in the economy's future.

Initial Jobless Claims

One of the most obvious indicators of economic problems is mass layoffs and long lines at unemployment offices around the country. Initial jobless claims is a statistic found in a report issued weekly by the U.S. Department of Labor. This number reveals how many people have reported for the first time that they have lost their job. This is an important number for economists to look at because it reveals the extent to which companies do not have the money necessary to keep their current staffing levels. The statistic does not reflect the total number of people who are receiving unemployment benefits from the federal government, but it does indicate the number of newly unemployed people in the United States.

When initial jobless claims suddenly spike or rise steadily, negative ripple effects often occur throughout the economy. Investors get nervous and possibly take money out of the stock market, fearing lower stock prices are ahead or even an all-out crash. Lower levels of investor interest leave companies with less money to spend, so even more layoffs become likely. Growing unemployment and loss of investment income among those Americans who are still working but also invest in the stock market put a major dent in consumer confidence.

Spending slows among consumers and businesses alike, and a recession takes hold.

When initial jobless claims begin to level off or decrease, investors feel renewed confidence in the job market and may decide to invest more money in stocks. As a result, companies are again flush with cash and resume hiring and spending on new products, research, and equipment. Consumer confidence bounces back, as does consumer spending. The economy is on the road to recovery.

During 2008, initial jobless claims topped six hundred thousand. In August of that year alone, eighty-four thousand jobs were lost. Companies continued to shed employees at alarming rates through 2009 and part of 2010. By the time the Great Recession ended, over eight million jobs had been lost. The leveling off of initial jobless claims is a good indicator for economists that the economy is again beginning to grow.

MYTHS and FACTS

MYTH If a company experiences mass layoffs, a recession is coming.

FACT One or two companies requiring mass layoffs to survive could be an indicator of poor planning instead of any economy-wide problems. The company may not have been managed properly and may have hired too many people to begin with. However, when mass layoffs occur among large numbers of companies across many different industries, the economy is most likely entering or is in the midst of a recession.

MYTH People can't control what happens in the economy, so they might as well spend money when they have it.

FACT It is important to save money for both retirement, future home purchases, a child's college tuition, and many other planned future expenditures. Money you spend now is money that won't be available for those important future needs. It's also a good idea to have the equivalent of at least one year's income in a savings account in order to create a hedge against prolonged unemployment.

MYTH Having a job throughout a recession means that a person does not have money problems.

FACT Even when a person has a job, recessions can bring higher prices for necessary items such as food and fuel. Many companies also cut down on people's work hours, wages, or salary and benefits during a recession.

CHAPTER THREE

COINCIDENT INDICATORS

When you think about all the leading indicators of an economy, it may seem like they are happening at the same time the economy shrinks or grows. But they really do happen a little bit ahead of the game for a lot of people.

Even though there may be shrinking sales of big-ticket items and a growing number of layoffs, the economy still functions for many people like it normally would. Although families may not be buying new cars or kitchen appliances at the moment, they are still buying food, clothing, and other necessities. They are even purchasing a few lower-price luxuries (like restaurant meals, haircuts, gym memberships, movie tickets, and MP3 downloads). Even those who have been laid off, are using their savings or unemployment insurance to participate in the economy by making necessary purchases. However, as an economy begins to shrink, the ripple effects will begin to negatively affect a larger and larger percentage of people in more serious ways.

INDUSTRIAL PRODUCTION

Industrial production is a measure of the total output of factories and mines in the United States. The data is released each month by the Federal Reserve Board. It is an indicator of economic performance because it directly relates to the number of orders being made for products or the number of products that companies think they can sell in the current economic environment.

As an economic indicator, industrial production is often linked to durable goods orders. This is because factories

Industrial production is a good indicator of the relative health of the economy. Even the production of something like coal indicates whether the economy is growing or shrinking. When the demand for power—and, therefore, the coal that supplies it—is high, companies have the money to manufacture more goods and fuel their operations.

adjust the number of products they make—they revise their production levels—once the number of orders for goods has changed. For example, if fewer people began buying cars a year ago, automakers would produce fewer cars this year, in order to bring their supply in line with consumer demand. Unsold cars from last year still crowd lots and showrooms around the country. Until that inventory is reduced, there is no need for large numbers of newly manufactured cars. In this way, industrial production is an economic indicator that manifests itself after initial changes have already started. It lags behind and reacts to the leading indicator of durable goods orders.

THE UNEMPLOYMENT RATE

In the wake of mass layoffs by businesses, people's incomes decrease dramatically—or even disappear—until they can find a new job. Many people file for unemployment benefits. The government will pay each unemployed person a certain amount of money each week to help him or her pay bills and meet expenses. This insurance was put into place after the Great Depression, when up to 25 percent of the country was unemployed and sank into poverty because of the lack of available jobs (during economic boom times, the unemployment rate might go as low as 4 percent). In this way, the government attempts to protect its citizens from being too severely affected by economic conditions that are beyond their control.

The rate of unemployment in the nation is an economic indicator that clearly reflects the current state of the economy.

In times of low unemployment, there are many jobs available and the economy is strong. In times of high unemployment, the economy is shrinking and possibly experiencing a recession or even a more severe depression. Unemployment leads to loss of income, which puts a halt to consumer spending. This reduced spending leads to lower profits for businesses, even more layoffs, and lower consumer confidence and spending. This is a recessionary spiral. Until money again begins circulating in the economy—through some kind of stimulus effort—it is very difficult to reverse.

Personal Income and Outlays

One important measure of the amount of money that people have to put back into the economy is Personal Income and Outlays. This report is compiled and released each month by the Bureau of Economic Analysis. It tracks people's personal income and monthly spending. This includes spending on durable goods and other consumer goods, such as food, clothing, entertainment, and home items.

Of course, the amount of income that someone has to spend depends on his or her employment situation. When people are unemployed or underemployed, their incomes shrink significantly. The amount of money that someone spends on daily or monthly living expenses is called his or her outlay. So someone who has no income or a severely diminished income may no longer be able to make mortgage or car payments, or pay the cell phone bill each month. He or she will have less to spend on groceries or home supplies for the family.

Counting the Unemployed

During the Great Recession, reports from the Bureau of Labor Statistics indicated that the unemployment rate rose to over 10 percent. However, many economists believe that the true unemployment rate was even higher than that. This is because the report does not account for people in various unique situations.

For example, the unemployment rate is based on the number of people collecting unemployment insurance. People who have given up looking for work so that they can take care of their families are not counted. People who have seasonal, part-time, or temporary jobs are not counted, even if they would prefer to have a full-time job but could not find one. These people are labeled "underemployed," which means that they once had better jobs but can no longer find employment at the same level that they once did. People who accept early retirement packages from their companies to avoid being laid off are also not counted in the unemployment figures. These people are characterized as "hidden unemployment" but are not measured in the unemployment rate.

It is believed by many economists that if all of these groups of people were included in the unemployment figures, the rate would have been closer to 20 percent than the 10 percent that was reported during the Great Recession.

Improving unemployment statistics do not always provide a full and accurate picture. Employment rates can get a boost from seasonal employment, such as farming, or temporary employment, such as salesclerking during the holiday retail season.

As people adjust their expenses in a tight economy, they may make a budget. A budget helps them determine what they can afford and keeps them from spending beyond their more limited means. This may mean sacrificing things they once took for granted, like dinners out, brand-name groceries and products at the supermarket (rather than discounted store brands), and premium cable television packages.

The overall measure of personal income in 2008 decreased by over $20 billion. That's a lot less money flowing through the economy from employers to employees and into the market-place (and then back to producers and employers via consumer purchases). As a result, people made radical adjustments to their spending. Personal consumption decreased by over $56 billion.

Consumer spending on nonessential goods and services is a good indication of how the economy is doing. A sure sign of economic improvement is when people have more money to spend on entertainment.

RETAIL SALES

During any holiday season, you may see a lot of people at the mall, but are they actually shopping? If so, are they purchasing goods at full price or at steep discounts? A monthly report on retail sales helps shed light on consumer spending patterns, thereby reflecting the current state of consumer confidence and the perceived health of the economy.

Retail sales typically improve when consumers feel more confident about their personal finances and the near future of the economy.

Reports of retail sales are a direct measure of the amount of money that people have to spend and how confident they feel about the economy. Each month, the Census Bureau and the Department of Commerce compile and release data about retail sales for the previous month. The data is compared to that of the previous month or the same month in the previous year.

Retail sales are a good indication of the economy's strength. Great sales mean a great economy. It means that people have money to spend and they feel confident about spending it. In recessionary times, the opposite is true. In 2008, retail sales plummeted because of the weakened economy and sharp recession. Sales were the worst they had been in thirty-five years. They continued to drop month by month for nearly a year.

CHAPTER FOUR
LAGGING INDICATORS

A recessionary period within the economic cycle can be long-lasting and painful for many businesses and individuals. Some recessions end quickly, while others endure for several years. Signs that the Great Recession of 2007–2009 was finally coming to an end gradually began to appear as economic indicators revealed signs of new life, even as most people still felt mired in the depths of the crisis.

As an economy heads out of recession, the economic indicators do not all point in the same direction. When an economic cycle ends, statistics may show an overall trend in one direction, but there may be some reports that show occasional sliding back in the opposite direction. For example, unemployment rates may begin to improve overall, but a certain week or month may reveal that a new round of unexpected layoffs has occurred. This can make investors and the general public nervous. They may doubt the strength of the economy or fear a "double-dip" recession, in which the economy experiences two recessions with a brief recovery in between. Yet the next month may show an increase in hiring and a decrease in new jobless claims, demonstrating that the economy is growing overall. This progress may be frustratingly slow and halting, however.

Though the economy may be in recovery, the average person may not be able to sense that. For him or her, times are still tough, and personal economic indicators have not yet picked up—employment, increased income, and the ability to purchase desired goods and services. If someone is still unemployed after a long period of time, for example, he or she may not be comforted by the statistics that say things are improving. Unless an individual, family, or company is experiencing the benefits of the improvement, there is little that can make them feel more at ease.

Economists, who collect and interpret data and statistics throughout the economic cycle to predict when improvements will take place, can offer some reassurance that things are indeed looking up. There are certain lagging indicators that occur in the wake of the movements of the economic cycle. These indicate and confirm that an economy has either entered a recovery and begun to experience renewed growth or has peaked and begun to experience contraction (shrinking) and perhaps recession.

CONSUMER PRICE INDEX

Each month, the Bureau of Labor Statistics releases the Consumer Price Index, a report detailing any changes in the prices that consumers are paying for goods and services. The index includes a representative sampling of various goods that many people buy and the services they normally spend money on. The index focuses on the buying habits of urban consumers because they make up about 87 percent of the total U.S. population.

The index includes food and beverages, such as cereal, milk, coffee, snacks, chicken, and wine. It also includes the money people spend on their homes, such as their rent and heating costs. Clothing, cars, gasoline, drug prescriptions, medical

A monthly report called the Consumer Price Index indicates if prices for common goods, such as gasoline, are generally rising or falling.

supplies, televisions, pet products, sports equipment, movie tickets, phone service, computer software, and even haircuts, tobacco products, and funeral expenses are all included in the Consumer Price Index.

The price index tracks the changes in these prices. The data is used to draw conclusions about the larger state of the economy. For example, if the price of a pair of jeans increased 10 percent in one year, but prices for most other goods and services increased only about 3 percent, it would seem to indicate that the economy was humming along normally. The economy was not subject to either harmful patterns of price inflation or deflation. The increase in the price of jeans may only be due to a spike in demand, a sudden drop-off in supply, an increase in labor costs, or a shortage of materials or manufacturing facilities. If, however, the Consumer Price Index indicated a roughly 10 percent increase in prices among many consumer products, that might indicate an overheating and inflationary economy. Similarly, a pronounced and widespread decrease in consumer prices would herald deflation and a recessionary economy.

PRODUCER PRICE INDEX

The Producer Price Index is another monthly report by the Bureau of Labor Statistics. It measures the average change over time in the prices that producers are paid for their goods. When an economy is suffering, a producer of goods will be happy to take any price it can get for its goods. This means that it lowers the price it charges wholesalers and retailers who buy its products. This lower wholesale price often gets passed on to the consumer as a lower retail price.

Producers will sometimes lower their prices even when the costs of production remain high. Their profits will decrease as a result. In a recession, there is a smaller gap between producer and consumer prices than there is in good economic times. A smaller gap between the two prices means a smaller profit margin for the producer. A larger gap indicates the producer is reaping greater profits by charging considerably more for a product than it cost to make. When producer prices remain fairly stable, rising only moderately, the economy has returned to an optimum level of performance.

Waiting for Results

Some of the statistics that are used to analyze the economy are released on a weekly basis. But many are released either monthly or each quarter of a year. Some are only released once a year. That means that good data on the changes in the economy do not come fast enough to create an accurate snapshot of what is happening right now.

Although the Great Recession was believed to have started in 2007, economists could not analyze the data and confirm that fact until well into 2008. That meant that many people were feeling the effects of the recession before it was even declared a recession. Similarly, it was not until September 2010 that it was confirmed and announced that the Great Recession had officially ended back in June 2009. Nevertheless, many people were still suffering the lingering effects of the recession. To them, it felt far from over.

LOANS AND RATES

When an economy is in bad shape, banks may offer low interest rates in order to stimulate it and increase consumer spending. Low interest rates make borrowing money less expensive and encourage consumers to take out large loans and buy big-ticket items, like houses and cars.

However, when an economy is in recovery or at its peak, banks are much more likely to charge higher interest rates. They assume that people have more income available to pay these higher rates. In addition, an economy that is well into a period of recovery or is at its peak is in danger of experiencing

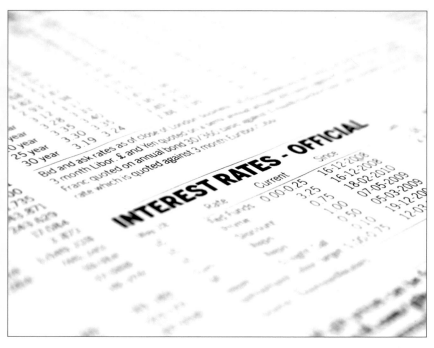

During a recession, interest rates are usually lowered to encourage consumers to borrow and spend more.

inflation—when too much money is in circulation. Charging higher interest rates helps drain the economy of some cash by discouraging borrowing. This helps cool an overheating economy, keeps prices steady, and can prolong the period between recessions.

Value of Outstanding Commercial and Industrial Loans

The Federal Deposit Insurance Corporation (FDIC) provides a banking report every quarter. In an improving economy, the number of loans held by the bank decreases. The number of defaults on loans and the incidence of foreclosures also decrease. This means that people can afford to pay off their loans (or meet their monthly payments), remain in their homes, and hold on to their business properties. When these numbers improve, it is a sign that the economy has as well.

Average Prime Interest Rate Charged by Banks

A prime interest rate is the interest that a bank charges its customers when they take out loans. These loans are taken out to buy expensive items, such as homes and cars. During a recession, this interest rate tends to be cut in order to stimulate borrowing and spending and thereby generate an economic revival. However, once the economy picks up, cash is again circulating, and consumer spending increases along with prices. At this point, the Federal Reserve tends to raise the prime interest rate again in order to curb inflation.

The prime rate is a lagging indicator because it is raised or lowered in reaction to what is being observed in the economy after most of the leading and coincident indicator data has already been gathered and analyzed. If a recession seems to be taking hold, the rate is lowered. If a recovery is seen to be underway, the rate is raised.

Manufacturing, Sales, and Hiring

Once an economy is in recovery, manufacturing activity and sales pick up, following the slump that accompanies a recession. At this point, the supply of manufactured goods will again be more in line with demand. Whereas in a recession unsold inventory tends to build up as consumer demand drops, in a recovery demand will clear out inventory and may even outstrip supply.

Consumer sales increase as people's income levels rise. As a result, companies can again begin producing more goods to keep up with the renewed demand. In some cases, this may mean hiring back a certain percent of employees whom the companies had let go during the recession. When hiring and job creation increase

consistently over time, the economy can be said to have truly entered a recovery.

Hiring is one of the last indicators of a recovering economy. This is because companies tend to operate with a reduced

As consumer confidence and spending increase following a recession, manufacturing and hiring also increase, creating a positive feedback cycle for the economy.

workforce in the early days of a recovery, before production levels and profits have fully returned to prerecession levels. Once a company is again producing at full capacity and has enjoyed rising profits for a period of time—using them to invest in new machines, facilities, and product development—it is again ready to hire additional employees.

Manufacturing and sales lead these employment booms. It takes people to make and manufacture goods. These working people then have the money to spend on the things they need. Their spending results in business profits, more production, and still more hiring, income increases, and consumer spending. A positive cycle has taken hold.

CHAPTER FIVE

LOOKING AHEAD

Economists are always looking toward the future. Their analysis of the past and current economic conditions can help them make predictions about what might be coming in the future.

In 2011, after years of struggling through hard economic times, leading, coincident, and lagging indicators all pointed to the fact that the Great Recession was over. In fact, it had ended in 2009, though the recovery was very slow. Consumer confidence began to rise tentatively, and consumer sales followed suit. Because people had curtailed spending and borrowing during the recession, their credit ratings had risen, while their debt load had decreased (though the debt and mortgage crises were by no means over). Manufacturing picked up, businesses expanded, and new stores opened where others had failed a few months before. The opening of new stores and the increase in manufacturing activity and consumer sales resulted in hiring and job creation, and unemployment levels slowly

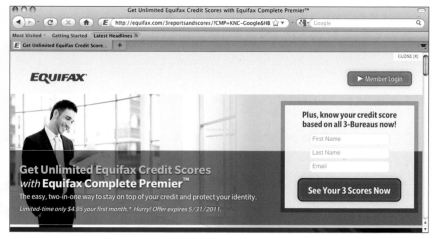

People who save money, limit and effectively manage their debt, and pay their bills on time generally have high credit scores. Having good credit allows them to borrow money to make large purchases, such as homes and cars.

began to sink. New construction, halted for most of the recession, resumed as money once again circulated throughout the economy.

ANTICIPATING AND IDENTIFYING THE NEXT BUBBLE

Even during boom times, many economists say that it is hard to detect where the next bubble will arise. The stock market bubble of the 1920s, the dot-com bubble of the late 1990s, and the real estate bubble of the early twenty-first century had already formed and were on the verge of bursting before they were recognized as being a major problem and well after anything could be done to avoid catastrophe.

Just like economists, average people can try to analyze and interpret economic indicators. It is not easy, but paying attention to the statistics that are released each week, month,

A division of the U.S. government called the Bureau of Labor and Statistics (http://www.bls.gov) collects and analyzes much of the data that we rely on to tell us how the economy is doing and how it will perform in the near future.

or quarter from the Bureau of Labor Statistics can help keep people informed about the economic climate around them. If first-time unemployment claims are rising week after week, or retail sales are falling month after month, a person can begin to see the leading indicators of a negative economic trend. He or she can then begin planning ahead for a likely period of reduced income and employment uncertainty.

UNEXPECTED EVENTS

What economists cannot predict or foresee are events that will change the direction of the economy unexpectedly, for good or bad. For example, the United States spent most of the 1930s in a deep depression. Despite all of the extraordinary efforts that were made to create jobs and protect the health and well-being

Unexpected events can drastically alter an economy's direction. One such event was the outbreak of World War II. The boost that war preparations gave to manufacturing finally pulled the United States out of a long depression.

of the most vulnerable citizens during the New Deal era, it was an unexpected event that finally ended the Great Depression—the entry of the United States into World War II.

The war required new businesses to spring up and old ones to again begin manufacturing. Equipment was needed for the war effort—weapons, ammunition, vehicles, planes, ships, uniforms, and food. Civilian industries had to manufacture and supply all of these goods—and quickly. Many new jobs were created virtually overnight. With so many men being shipped overseas to fight, there were more jobs than there were available workers. This is when women first entered the U.S. workforce in large numbers.

While the United States spent more during the war than it had on hand—and therefore went into debt—the stimulation to the economy helped put an end to the Great Depression. All of the leading indicators pointed to a new boom time, driven by the war effort.

Manufacturing was up, as was employment. Investors who bought stocks of companies that supplied the war effort were making huge returns on their investments. Orders for durable goods were sky-high. These included weapons, ammunition, airplanes, cars, and just about anything else that was ordered for the troops abroad. International trade and transactions with allies in the war effort were also booming at this time. All of the leading indicators showed that the economy had come back to roaring life.

Postwar Boom

The economic activity associated with the war effort was bound to come to an end once the fighting ceased and peacetime returned. Many people feared that the sudden end to wartime manufacturing, coupled with the return of millions of servicemen in need of work, would send the country back into a recessionary cycle. Yet, against these expectations, another economic boom occurred.

The manufacturing boom of World War II and high levels of postwar consumer spending brought unprecedented prosperity to the United States during most of the 1950s.

The United States ended the war as a newly confident super-power nation, while most of Europe was devastated physically, economically, and emotionally. Flush with victory and renewed confidence following the end of both a depression and the deprivations of war, Americans had a lot of pent-up consumer energy. They were ready to spend.

Americans had been scrimping, saving, and sacrificing since 1929—almost twenty years. As they emerged from this long period of darkness and self-denial, a huge demand developed for products and goods that fueled economic growth. These included homes in the newly created suburbs, appliances, electronics, and furniture for these new homes, and cars for their new garages. Manufacturing in the United States continued to rise throughout the remainder of the 1940s and most of the 1950s.

LOOKING FOR THE NEXT BOOM

Many economists agree that the United States needs some sort of manufacturing boom to help fuel the economy in the wake of the Great Recession. One area of the economy that may lead to a boom is the alternative energy industry. When Americans make the switch from fossil fuels to renewable and green energy sources, a lot of manufacturing work will need to be done to create new energy infrastructure,

The next manufacturing boom in the United States may result from the switch to alternative energy sources and away from a reliance on fossil fuels.

systems, and appliances. It will change the way that buildings and homes are constructed and how they receive, store, generate, and use energy to power their operations. It will change the kinds of cars that are built and the service stations that supply energy or fuel.

No matter what it is that creates an economic boom, there will always be ripple effects throughout the economy. And every boom eventually ends in a bust. Anticipating, preparing for, and making the most of both boom and bust times, recessions and recoveries, requires familiarity with and an understanding of economic indicators and an ability to interpret what they say about the economy's—and one's own—near future.

Ten Great Questions
to Ask a Financial Adviser

1. What kind of job is always needed, even during a recession?

2. Where can I keep my money during a recession so that it always earns interest or otherwise grows?

3. How can I benefit from a boom economy?

4. How can I cut down my expenses so that my money lasts longer?

5. How much money should a person save in case of job loss?

6. How should I decide whether or not to put off major expenditures, like a vacation or new computer?

7. Should a person sell his or her stock if it has lost a lot of value?

8. Why do some people buy more stock during a recession?

9. What is the best way to save a lot of money both in the short term and in the long term?

10. How do I plan my finances if I'm struggling in good times or doing well in bad times?

GLOSSARY

budget An estimate of what will be earned and what will be spent during a certain period.

coincident economic indicator Data regarding economic conditions or activities that reflect the present state of the economy, rather than its past or likely future states.

Consumer Confidence Index A statistical measure of how people feel about where the economy is headed. A high confidence index usually coincides with higher levels of consumer spending, and vice versa.

Consumer Sentiment Index A monthly index that measures peoples' attitudes about the economy and their own personal finances.

debt Money that is owed to another person or group after it has been borrowed.

durable good An item that does not wear out quickly and thus does not need to be replaced very often.

economic indicators Statistics and data that give economists clues about the direction the economy is going in and its relative health.

Federal Reserve The central bank of the United States that dictates the nation's monetary policies, primarily by using interest rates to control the money supply and prevent both deflation and inflation.

foreclosure The repossession of property by a bank after the owner has failed to meet monthly loan payments.

gross domestic product (GDP) The total value of goods and services produced within a country during a given period of time, usually a year. The GDP of the United States is measured both quarterly (four times a year) and annually (at year's end).

inflation An increase in the cost of goods and services.

inventory The exact number of particular items in a store or a warehouse.

lagging economic indicator Data regarding economic conditions or activities that manifest themselves after the major movements of the economic cycle. This indicator is one that becomes apparent only after the economy has emerged into a new phase of the business cycle. It reflects the economy's previous position in that cycle.

leading economic indicator Data regarding economic conditions or activities that precede movements of the economic cycle. These conditions or activities change before the economy as a whole changes.

prime interest rate The interest rate that a bank charges a customer for taking out a loan.

Producer Price Index A monthly report that measures the average change over time in the prices that producers are paid for their goods.

recession An economic downturn, usually defined as six months or more of declining value of a nation's goods and services. A recession is typically characterized by unemployment, low consumer and business spending, and a lack of money circulating throughout the economy.

FOR MORE INFORMATION

Bureau of Economic Analysis (BEA)
1441 L Street NW
Washington, DC 20230
(202) 606-9900
Web site: http://www.bea.gov
Part of the Department of Commerce, the BEA
    produces accounts statistics on the American
    economy.

Canadian Economics Association (CEA)
CP 8888 Succursale Centre-Ville
Montréal, QC H3C 3P8
Canada
(514) 987-3000, ext. 8374
Web site: http://economics.ca
The CEA is an organization of about 1,500 economists in
    Canada.

Department of Finance Canada
140 O'Connor Street
Ottawa, ON K1A 0G5
Canada
(613) 992-1573

Web site: http://www.fin.gc.ca
The Department of Finance Canada oversees the Canadian
government's budget and spending.

Jump$tart Coalition for Personal Financial Literacy
919 18th Street NW, Suite 300
Washington, DC 20006
(888) 45-EDUCATE [338-2283]
Web site: http://www.jumpstart.org
The Jump$tart Coalition is a nonprofit partnership of
many national organizations that support financial
education or provide tools for teaching financial
education.

Junior Achievement
1 Education Way
Colorado Springs, CO 80906
(719) 540-8000
Web site: http://www.ja.org
Junior Achievement is the world's largest organization for
educating students about financial literacy through
hands-on programs.

National Council on Economic Education (NCEE)
122 East 42nd Street, Suite 2600
New York, NY 10168
(212) 730-7007
Web site: http://www.councilforeducation.org
The NCEE is a nationwide network that promotes economic
literacy for students and their teachers.

National Endowment for Financial Education (NEFE)
1331 17th Street, Suite 1200
Denver, CO 80202
(303) 741-6333
Web site: http://www.nefe.org
The NEFE is a national nonprofit foundation dedicated to
helping Americans control their own finances.

U.S. Bureau of Labor Statistics (BLS)
Postal Square Building
2 Massachusetts Avenue NE
Washington, DC 20212-0001
(202) 691-5200
Web site: http://www.bls.gov
The BLS is the principal federal agency responsible for
measuring labor market activity, working conditions, and
price changes in the economy. Its mission is to collect,
analyze, and disseminate essential economic information
to support public and private decision making.

WEB SITES

Due to the changing nature of Internet links, Rosen
Publishing has developed an online list of Web sites related to
the subject of this book. This site is updated regularly. Please
use this link to access the list:

http://www.rosenlinks.com/rwe/eind

FOR FURTHER READING

Acton, Johnny, and David Goldblatt. *Economy*. New York, NY: DK, 2010.

Andrews, Carolyn. *Economics in Action*. New York, NY: Crabtree Publishing, 2008

Craats, Rennay. *Economy: USA Past Present Future*. New York, NY: Weigl Publishers, 2009.

Gale Group. *The U.S. Economy*. Farmington Hills, MI: Gale Cengage Learning, 2010.

Gilman, Laura Anne. *Economics*. Minneapolis, MN: Lerner Publications, 2006.

Gorman, Tom. *The Complete Idiot's Guide to the Great Recession*. New York, NY: Penguin Group, 2010.

Hall, Alvin. *Show Me the Money: How to Make Cents of Economics*. New York, NY: DK, 2008.

Jewler, Sue. *Making Sense of Economics*. Hawthorne, NJ: Educational Impressions, 2006.

Merino, Noel. *The World Economy* (Current Controversies). San Diego, CA: Greenhaven Press, 2010.

Miller Debra A. *The U.S. Economy* (Current Controversies). San Diego, CA: Greenhaven Press, 2010.

Thomas, Lloyd B. *The Financial Crisis and Federal Reserve Policy*. New York, NY: Palgrave Macmillan, 2011.

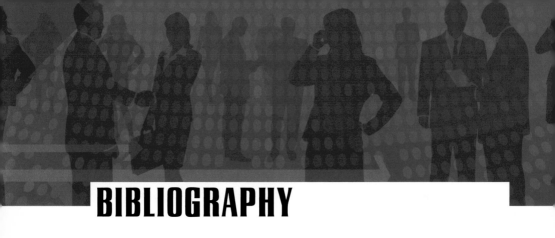

BIBLIOGRAPHY

Baumohl, Bernard. *The Secrets of Economic Indicators*. 2nd ed. Upper Saddle River, NJ: Wharton School Publishing, 2008.

Blaine, Charley. "Wall Street Says 'Good Riddance!' to 2008." MSN.com, December 31, 2008. Retrieved February 2011 (http://articles.moneycentral.msn.com/Investing/Dispatch/worst-year-since-1931-123108.aspx).

Censky, Annalyn. "Consumer Confidence Slumps in September." CNN.com, September 28, 2010. Retrieved February 2011 (http://money.cnn.com/2010/09/28/news/economy/consumer_confidence/index.htm).

Christie, Les. "Foreclosures Spike 112%— No End in Sight." CNN.com, April 29, 2008. Retrieved February 2011 (http://money.cnn.com/2008/04/29/real_estate/foreclosures_still_rising/index.htm?postversion=2008042909).

Christie, Les. "Foreclosures Up 75% in 2007." CNN.com, January 29, 2008. Retrieved February 2011 (http://money.cnn.com/2008/01/29/real_estate/foreclosure_filings_2007).

Christie, Les. "Foreclosures: 'Worst Three Months of All Time.'" CNN.com, October 15, 2009. Retrieved February 2011 (http://money.cnn.com/2009/10/15/real_estate/foreclosure_crisis_deepens).

Clifford, Catherine. "Consumer Confidence: Worst Since '92." CNN.com, May 27, 2008. Retrieved February 2011 (http://money.cnn.com/2008/05/27/news/economy/consumer_confidence/?postversion=2008052713).

EconoIndicators.com. "Personal Income and Spending at a Glance." November 2008. Retrieved February 2011 (http://econoindicators.com/2008/12/personal-income-outlays-november-2008).

The Economist. *Guide to Global Economic Indicators*. Hoboken, NJ: John Wiley & Sons, 1992.

Fox, Eric. "Commercial and Industrial Loan Defaults Rise." Investopedia.com, March 10, 2009. Retrieved February 2011 (http://stocks.investopedia.com/stock-analysis/2009/commercial-and-industrial-loan-defaults-rise-cma-umbf-bokf-cfr-sivb0310.aspx).

Frumkin, Norman. *Guide to Economic Indicators*. 3rd ed. Armonk, NY: M. E. Sharpe, 2000.

Gammeltoft, Nikolaj. "Most U.S. Stocks Drop as S&P 500 Gains 13% in Second Straight Annual Rally." Bloomberg.com, December 31, 2010. Retrieved February 2011 (http://www.bloomberg.com/news/2010-12-31/u-s-stock-index-futures-fluctuate-s-p-500-is-poised-for-annual-advance.html).

Goldman, David. "Jobless Claims Soar Near 7-Year High." CNN.com, September 25, 2008. Retrieved February 2011 (http://money.cnn.com/2008/09/25/news/economy/jobless_claims).

Isidore, Chris. "Februrary Jobs Report: Unemployment Falls Again." CNN.com, March 4, 2011. Retrieved March 2011 (http://money.cnn.com/2011/03/04/news/economy/february_jobs_report/index.htm?hpt=Sbin).

McAbby, Matt. "Is the Consumer Confident?" Jutia Group, January 14, 2009. Retrieved February 2011 (http://jutiagroup.com/20090114-is-the-consumer-confident).

Moffatt, Mike. "A Beginner's Guide to Economic Indicators." About.com. Retrieved February 2011 (http://economics.about.com/cs/businesscycles/a/economic_ind.htm).

Moffatt, Mike. "Why Don't Prices Decline During a Recession?: The Link Between the Business Cycle and Inflation." About.com. Retrieved February 2011 (http://economics.about.com/cs/money/a/recession_price.htm).

Rampell, Catherine. "Average Length of Unemployment Reaches High." *New York Times*, March 4, 2011. Retrieved March 2011 (http://economix.blogs.nytimes.com/2011/03/04/average-length-of-unemployment-reaches-high-of-37-1-weeks).

Rooney, Ben. "Consumer Confidence Plummets." CNN.com, February 24, 2009. Retrieved February 2011 (http://money.cnn.com/2009/02/24/news/economy/consumer_confidence).

Rosenbloom, Stephanie. "Retail Sales Are Weakest in 35 Years." *New York Times*, December 4, 2008. Retrieved February 2011 (http://www.nytimes.com/2008/12/05/business/economy/05shop.html).

The Star Online. "Wall St. Closes Out 2009 with Best Gains Since 2003." January 2, 2010. Retrieved February 2011 (http://biz.thestar.com.my/news/story.asp?file=/2010/1/2/business/5402401&sec=business).

INDEX

About the Author

Kathy Furgang is a writer and editor who has written previously on economic subjects, including the national debt, budget deficits, and the stock market.

Photo Credits

Cover (housing construction), p. 1 (lower right) © www.istockphoto.com/Justin Horrocks; cover (headline) © www.istockphoto.com/Lilli Day; pp. 5, 8–9, 12–13,17, 52, 54–55, 64–65 Shutterstock; pp. 7, 16, 38, 47, 57 from photo by Mario Tama/Getty Images; pp. 14, 59 Bureau of Labor Statistics; p. 18–19 Joe Raedle/Getty Images; p. 21 Bill Pugliano/Getty Images; pp. 26–27 Kevork Djansezian/Getty Images; pp. 28–29 Spencer Platt/Getty Images; pp. 30–31 Brian Kersey/Getty Images; p. 39 Bloomberg/Bloomberg via Getty Images; pp. 42–43 Jerry Alexander/The Image Bank/Getty Images; p. 44 Chris Hondros/Getty Images; p. 45 Fuse/Getty Images; pp. 48–49 Justin Sullivan/Getty Images; p. 58 © 2011 Equifax; pp. 60–61 Hulton Archive/Archive Photos/Getty Images; pp. 62–63 A. Y. Owen/Time & Life Pictures/Getty Images; cover and interior graphic elements: © www.istockphoto.com/Andrey Prokhorov (front cover), © www.istockphoto.com/Dean Turner (back cover and interior pages); www.istockphoto.com/Darja Tokranova (p. 37); www.istockphoto.com/articular (p. 67); © www.istockphoto.com/studiovision (pp. 68, 71, 75. 76, 79); © www.istockphoto.com/Chen Fu Soh (multiple interior pages).

Designer: Nicole Russo
Photo Researcher: Marty Levick

FRIENDS FREE LIBRARY
GERMANTOWN FRIENDS LIBRARY
5418 Germantown Avenue
Philadelphia, PA 19144
215-951-2355

Each borrower is responsible for all items
checked out on his/her library card, for
fines on materials kept overtime, and
replacing any lost or damaged materials.